THE STANLEY CUP FINALS

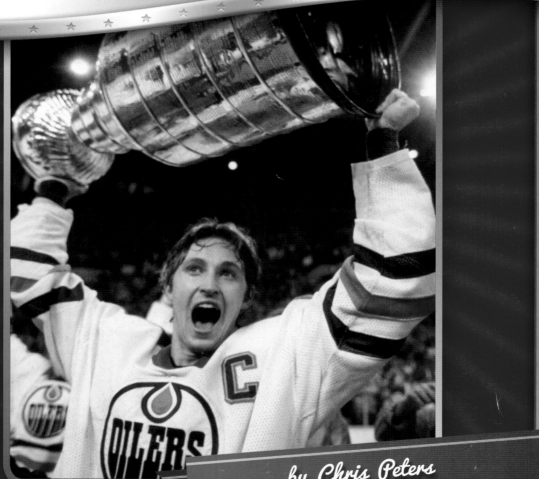

by Chris Peters

Published by ABDO Publishing Company, PO Box 398166, Minneapolis, MN 55439. Copyright © 2013 by Abdo Consulting Group, Inc. International copyrights reserved in all countries. No part of this book may be reproduced in any form without written permission from the publisher. SportsZone™ is a trademark and logo of ABDO Publishing Company.

Printed in the United States of America,
North Mankato, Minnesota
112012
012013

 THIS BOOK CONTAINS AT LEAST 10% RECYCLED MATERIALS.

Editor: Chrös McDougall
Series Designer: Craig Hinton

Photo Credits: The Canadian Press/Frank Gunn/AP Images, cover, 9; Bruce Bennett Studios/Getty Images, title, 17, 25, 60 (center); Gene J. Puskar/AP Images, 5; The Canadian Press/Andrew Vaughan/AP Images, 11, 59 (bottom, right); Universal History Archive/Getty Images, 13; Transcendental Graphics/Getty Images, 18; The Canadian Press/Steve White/AP Images, 21, 58 (top, left); AP Images, 28, 31, 33, 37, 41, 58 (top, right), 59 (top); A.E. Maloof/AP Images, 39; Focus on Sport/Getty Images, 45, 58 (bottom); David E. Klutho/Sports Illustrated/Getty Images, 47; Ron Frehm/AP Images, 49, 59 (bottom, left); Brian K. Diggs/AP Images, 51; David Zalubowski/AP Images, 55; The Canadian Press/Jonathan Hayward/AP Images, 57; Tom Hevezi/AP Images, 60 (top); Rick Bowmer/AP Images, 60 (bottom)

Cataloging-in-Publication Data
Peters, Chris.
The Stanley Cup Finals / Chris Peters.
   p. cm. -- (Sports' great championships)
Includes bibliographical references and index.
ISBN 978-1-61783-672-5
1. Hockey--History--Juvenile literature. 2. Stanley Cup (Hockey)--Juvenile literature. I. Title.
796.962--dc22

                                                    2012946326

TABLE OF CONTENTS

The Most Famous Trophy

Expectations were always high for Sidney Crosby. In 2003, *Sports Illustrated* featured the then 16-year-old and called him "The Next One." That was in reference to Wayne Gretzky, who was known as "The Great One" during his career in the 1980s and 1990s.

"He's the best player I've seen since Mario [Lemieux]," Gretzky said, referring to another legendary player.

Those expectations only grew when the Pittsburgh Penguins drafted Crosby first in the 2005 National Hockey League (NHL) Draft. To live up to

Pittsburgh Penguins 21-year-old captain Sidney Crosby takes a break during practice prior to Game 7 of the 2009 Stanley Cup Finals.

How to Win the Cup

The Stanley Cup is awarded to the winner of the NHL's Stanley Cup playoffs. As of 2012, there were 30 teams in the NHL. After 82 regular-season games, 16 teams make the playoffs. Half come from the Eastern Conference and half come from the Western Conference.

The NHL postseason is one of the most grueling in all of sports. It usually lasts approximately six weeks, from April to June. Every playoff series is a best-of-seven format. So the first team to win four games advances to the next round. The last team standing in the East meets the winner from the West in the Stanley Cup Finals.

The winner of the Western Conference Finals receives the Clarence S. Campbell Bowl. It is named for the NHL president who served from 1946 to 1977. The winner of the Eastern Conference Finals takes home the Prince of Wales Trophy. It is named for the British monarch who donated the trophy to the NHL in 1924.

the expectations, Crosby would have to follow Gretzky and Lemieux in winning hockey's ultimate prize: the Stanley Cup. Crosby nearly did so in 2008. He led the Penguins to the Stanley Cup Finals only to lose in six games to the Detroit Red Wings.

It was an amazing turnaround for a team that had missed the playoffs every year from 2002 to 2006. But the Penguins still needed to take that last step. History was in danger of repeating itself in 2009. The Penguins and Red Wings met again in the Stanley Cup Finals. But Detroit won the first two games.

History was not on Pittsburgh's side. Only three

Stanley's Many Shapes and Sizes

The Stanley Cup has taken many shapes and sizes over the years. But it has held its current shape since about 1950. The Stanley Cup is the only trophy in professional team sports that inscribes the names of the players who win. So naturally it has run out of room. Therefore, the Hockey Hall of Fame began retiring bands in 1992. That way the Cup could maintain the shape people have grown familiar with. Also, the Cup that is presented now is merely a replica of the one Lord Frederick Arthur Stanley purchased in 1892. The original remains on display, with the retired bands, at the Hockey Hall of Fame in Toronto.

teams had ever come back to win the Stanley Cup after losing the first two games. The last time it happened was nearly 40 years prior. The good news for the Penguins, however, was that the series was shifting back to Pittsburgh for games 3 and 4.

The home-ice advantage must have worked, too. The Penguins won both games 4–2. Crosby scored what stood to be the game-winning goal in Game 4. But the veteran Red Wings bounced back in Game 5. They needed just one more win to again lift the Stanley Cup.

Just like the year before, the Penguins were on home ice for Game 6. Only this time, the Stanley Cup stayed in its case. After a scoreless first period, the Penguins scored a goal early in each of the second and third periods. The 2–1 Penguins victory forced Game 7 in Detroit.

Game 7

Game 7 was an intense battle from the moment the puck dropped. The first period ended in a 0–0 deadlock. Then the Penguins got a spark in the second from a somewhat unexpected source.

Center Maxime Talbot was known more for his grit and toughness than skill. But he showed some offensive flair just 1:13 into the second period. Penguins center Evgeni Malkin's skate deflected an attempted clearing pass by Detroit directly to Talbot. Talbot then surprised Detroit goalie Chris Osgood with a quick shot. Pittsburgh went up 1–0.

Pittsburgh's high soon turned to a low. Detroit's Johan Franzen drove Crosby into the boards. Crosby's left leg was pinned between the big Detroit forward's body and the boards. A knee injury left Crosby unable to skate. Pittsburgh would have to play the entire last half of the game without its captain and best player.

Losing Crosby was sure to be a huge blow. But Talbot came through once again. Just halfway through the second period, he placed a beautiful wrist shot over the outstretched glove of Osgood. It went into the upper-right corner of the net for a 2–0 Pittsburgh lead.

Heading into the third period, the Penguins were just 20 minutes away from the Stanley Cup. Then a Detroit goal with 6:07 to play made

Pittsburgh Penguins center Maxime Talbot sends a shot past Detroit Red Wings goalie Chris Osgood during Game 7 of the 2009 Stanley Cup Finals.

it 2–1. Time continued to tick down. The Penguins inched ever closer to the ultimate prize. Detroit simply would not give up, though.

The Red Wings did get one more chance to tie the game. Detroit's legendary captain Nicklas Lidstrom had what appeared to be an open look at the net. Lidstrom snapped a shot from the left side. But Penguins goalie Marc-Andre Fleury lunged from his left to his right. He got a piece of the puck with his blocker with just 1.1 seconds remaining. As the puck skittered away, the buzzer sounded.

The Pittsburgh Penguins had started the series with two losses. They had to play Game 7 on the road. They had to play most of the game

Traveling Trophy

The Hockey Hall of Fame in Toronto has a special area in which the Stanley Cup can be displayed. But the trophy is on the road nearly 300 days each year. In the NHL offseason, each player and staff member of the Stanley Cup-winning team gets to spend a day with the trophy. The Cup has been everywhere from Alaska to Florida to Japan to London, England, to Moscow, Russia. It has also made numerous appearances on television shows, movies, and commercials.

without their best player. But they had overcome the odds and won the Stanley Cup.

Crosby was still nursing his injury. But as team captain it was his honor to accept Lord Stanley's Cup from the NHL commissioner. So he did, and he lifted it high above his head—just as other hockey legends had done for more than a century.

The Celebration

Crosby was at home in Cole Harbour, Nova Scotia, that August. It was his twenty-second birthday. But perhaps more important, it was Crosby's day with the Stanley Cup. This time Crosby raised the Cup in front of his friends and neighbors in Cole Harbour. According to estimates, between 65,000 and 75,000 people came to celebrate with Crosby.

Crosby spent the day touring around his small hometown with the Cup. Then he and his childhood friends played a street hockey game at the local tennis courts. It was just as they had done many nights as kids. However this time, instead of playing for the imaginary Stanley Cup like those summer nights of long ago, they played for the real thing. Crosby and his team successfully "defended" the Cup.

"Individually, you think back to all the people who have helped you get to this point," Crosby said. "They all have a hand in it, whether it was a midget hockey coach or a teacher. It's almost like a way to say thanks. Having them see you lift the Cup and achieve your goal, they can feel a part of it, too."

Lord Stanley's Silver Bowl

Hockey as we know it today traces back to March 3, 1875. That is when Canadian James Creighton organized the first known game to be played under a roof. The game was played in Montreal, Quebec. Soon it took off across Canada.

Athletic clubs across Canada organized hockey teams. They competed against other local teams. Hockey soon became a spectator sport. Large crowds began attending games.

Frederick Arthur Stanley, also known as Lord Stanley, donated the Dominion Challenge Trophy in 1892. Today it is known as the Stanley Cup.

In 1888, England's Queen Victoria named Frederick Arthur Stanley, Lord of Preston, as Governor General of Canada. That winter he attended his first ice hockey game at the Montreal Winter Carnival. It included the Montreal Victorias playing against the Montreal Amateur Athletic Association (AAA). Lord Stanley and his family took a liking to hockey almost immediately.

Creating the Cup

Hockey competition at the time remained regional. Teams competed for local and regional championships. Lord Stanley came up with an idea to change that in 1892. He suggested that there should be a championship for teams across Canada.

Lord Stanley took his idea to the Ottawa Athletic Association in March of that year. He sent a top aide to make the pitch. The aide, Lord

Kilcoursie, read a letter written by Stanley. "I have for some time been thinking that it would be a good thing if there were a challenge cup which should be held from year to year by the champion hockey team in the dominion," Stanley wrote.

The people at the Ottawa Athletic Association agreed. Lord Stanley purchased a silver bowl from a silversmith in England. He called it the Dominion Challenge Trophy. Lord Stanley created the first rules for the Cup. He also appointed two men to be trustees to ensure the rules of the trophy were obeyed.

Sheriff John Sweetland and Philip D. Ross were the

Lord Stanley

His name has become famous around the world for its connection to the silver cup. But Lord Frederick Arthur Stanley was quite an important man in his time. At one point his father, the Earl of Derby, served as the prime minister of Britain. As a result, Lord Stanley quickly began a career in politics. In 1888, Queen Victoria appointed him the governor general of Canada. Canada was a dominion of the British Empire at the time. The governor general served as the queen's non-political representative in Canada.

Lord Stanley's term as governor general was cut slightly short. He was forced to return to England to assume the title of Earl of Derby after his brother died. Lord Stanley left Canada in July of 1893. He never saw a Stanley Cup game. However, Lord Frederick Arthur Stanley, Earl of Derby, was one of the first people inducted into the Hockey Hall of Fame in 1945.

first Stanley Cup trustees. They made sure the tournament was open to all amateur teams across Canada. That way it could truly be the Canadian hockey championship.

The trustees determined that the champion of the Amateur Hockey Association of Canada (AHAC) would start with the Challenge Trophy. After that, teams from outside the AHAC could challenge for the trophy. The only requirement for challengers was that they were champions of their own leagues.

First Champions

The Montreal AAA claimed the Dominion Challenge Trophy first. The team finished 7–1–0 in the AHAC's first season in 1893. Other champions from across Canada were free to challenge for the trophy. None did, however. So the Montreal AAA held onto the trophy until the end of the next season. Then it won the trophy again. The Montreal AAA beat the Montreal Victorias and the Ottawa Capitals to keep the trophy in 1894.

The earliest history of the Stanley Cup focused on eastern Canada. The sport was spreading west, though. In 1896, a team from Winnipeg, Manitoba, issued the first challenge. The Winnipeg Victorias had won the Manitoba Hockey League. That gave them the right to challenge the reigning champions.

The Winnipeg Victorias met the Montreal Victorias in February 1896. Winnipeg won 2–0. That made it the first team to successfully win a trophy challenge game. Winnipeg also became the first team from outside Quebec to be crowned champion of Canada.

The Winnipeg Victorias did not hold the trophy for long. The Montreal Victorias challenged Winnipeg the following December. The Montreal team reclaimed the trophy with a 6–5 win.

For the next 10 years, the Cup changed hands numerous times. Sometimes it changed hands twice in one year. During that time, more

The original Ottawa Senators, shown in 1906, were Stanley Cup champions 11 times from 1903 to 1927.

teams and leagues kept popping up across Canada. Teams from 18 different eligible leagues battled for the Stanley Cup at different points in its early history.

Professional Movement

There were more teams and players than ever before. Professional baseball was taking shape around that time in the United States. The idea of having professional hockey in Canada began to gain support, too.

The Montreal Wanderers pushed to allow professionals in 1906. By 1910, the professional National Hockey Association (NHA) was born. The Pacific Coast Hockey Association (PCHA) formed the following year out west. The PCHA included teams from both western Canada and the northwestern United States.

In 1915, the Stanley Cup trustees decided to abandon the challenge format. In addition, they declared that US teams were now eligible to win the Stanley Cup. The champion from the NHA would meet the champion from the PCHA in a postseason series. It somewhat resembled baseball's World Series. The first team to win three games in the series would win the Stanley Cup. The winner would no longer be declared champion of Canada. Now the winner would be considered world champion.

However, World War I raged in Europe from 1914 to 1918. Owners struggled to maintain their teams as it did. After the 1916–17 season, the NHA folded. But the dream of a professional hockey league was still alive. The owners of the remaining teams met at the Windsor Hotel in Montreal. They agreed to band together and form a new league.

They called it the National Hockey League.

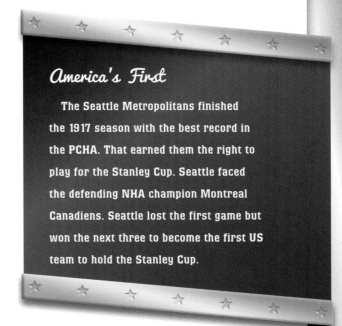

America's First

The Seattle Metropolitans finished the 1917 season with the best record in the PCHA. That earned them the right to play for the Stanley Cup. Seattle faced the defending NHA champion Montreal Canadiens. Seattle lost the first game but won the next three to become the first US team to hold the Stanley Cup.

The National Hockey League

B ack in 1917, few likely could have envisioned the NHL would develop into what it is today. World War I had made it difficult to run a team. Money was tight. Many young men were called into military service. But the remaining owners were determined to make the new league last.

The NHL basically replaced the NHA. Its champion would face the PCHA champion for the Stanley Cup. The first NHL-PCHA meeting came

The original Stanley Cup, first awarded in 1893, is now on display at the Hockey Hall of Fame in Toronto.

Stanley Gets the Flu

Since 1893, there have been only two years in which the Stanley Cup was not awarded. The first was in 1919. The NHL's Montreal Canadiens and PCHA's Seattle Metropolitans were deadlocked after five games. Each team had won twice. One game ended in a tie. At the time, many people in Seattle were getting sick with the Spanish Flu. Even some players were getting sick. Seattle health officials decided to cancel the series before a deciding sixth game could be played. No winner was declared. The only other year without a Stanley Cup champion was 2005. The 2004–05 NHL season was cancelled due to labor disagreements.

in 1918. The NHL's Toronto Arenas beat the Vancouver Millionaires three games to two.

Still, no single league was superior like the NHL is today. So in 1921, the Western Canada Hockey League (WCHL) formed. That meant three different leagues could compete for the Stanley Cup in 1921–22. The WCHL and PCHA were both West Coast leagues. So the trustees determined their champions would meet in a playoff. The winner would go on to play the NHL champion.

It did not matter much. The NHL consisted of only three or four teams from eastern Canada in its early seasons. Yet NHL teams won every Stanley Cup from 1918 to 1924. An early version of the Ottawa Senators won three titles. Meanwhile, the Montreal Canadiens won in 1924. That team still exists in the NHL today.

Finally the WCHL's Victoria Cougars won the 1925 Stanley Cup. They beat the Canadiens three games to one. No one could have known it at the time, but Victoria would be the last non-NHL team to lift the Stanley Cup as champions.

The NHL Takes Over

From its beginning, the NHL was an all-Canadian league. But league leaders, especially NHL president Frank Calder, knew it could not stay that way. League officials began seeking out businessmen to buy teams for large US cities. They believed that type of growth was needed for the league to survive.

A businessman named Charles Weston Adams attended a 1924 Stanley Cup game between the Canadiens and the WCHL's Calgary Tigers. It was there that NHL officials convinced him to buy a team. So in 1924–25, Adams's Boston Bruins debuted in the NHL.

Before the next season, the NHL sold the struggling Hamilton Tigers to William V. Dwyer. He moved the team to New York City and renamed it the Americans. Another NHL team debuted in Pittsburgh that season as well, giving the league seven teams.

A Tradition is Born

The Montreal Wanderers became the first team to engrave their players' names on the Stanley Cup in 1907. That act did not become an annual tradition until 1924. The Montreal Canadiens won their first Stanley Cup as an NHL team that year. By 2012 there were more than 2,000 names scrawled on the Stanley Cup. Only four people over the 120 years of the Cup's existence had served as the official engraver.

The PCHA and WCHL, meanwhile, were losing teams. They became no match for the growing NHL. The PCHA had ceased to exist after the 1923–24 season. The NHL's Montreal Maroons beat the WCHL's Victoria Cougars for the 1925–26 Stanley Cup. After that, the WCHL (then known as the WHL) ceased operations. That made the NHL the only true professional league in North America.

As a result, the Stanley Cup trustees granted sole rights of the Stanley Cup to the NHL. It was at this point that the NHL most began to resemble the dominant league it is today.

The league was up to 10 teams in 1926–27. Chicago businessman Major Frederic McLaughlin had bought the PCHA's Portland Rosebuds and moved them to his hometown. He renamed it the Black Hawks (they

NHL president Frank Calder presents the New York Rangers the Stanley Cup in 1933 after they defeated the Toronto Maple Leafs.

later became the Blackhawks). Out in New York City, a man named Tex Rickard convinced the league and the arena owners that the city could support another team. With that, the New York Rangers were born. Another US team was founded in Detroit. It later became the Detroit Red Wings in 1932. And up in Canada, the Toronto St. Patricks were due to be sold and moved to Philadelphia. Then native Ontarian Conn Smythe moved in and bought the club. He kept the team in Toronto and gave it a new name: the Maple Leafs. Those four teams from 1926–27—along with the Canadiens and Bruins—remain in the NHL today.

Silver Fox to the Rescue

New York Rangers coach Lester Patrick was in a bind. His team was facing the Montreal Maroons in the 1928 Stanley Cup Finals. New York's Lorne Chabot suffered a severe cut near his eye halfway through Game 2. Goalies did not wear masks at the time. But Patrick, known as the "Silver Fox" for his grey hair, had no one to replace the star goaltender. So the 44-year-old Patrick strapped on the goalie pads himself. The former defenseman allowed only one goal. New York went on to win the game 2–1 in overtime.

Patrick performed well in his first goaltending stint. It proved to be his last, though. New York received permission from the NHL to use Joe Miller of the New York Americans to finish the series in goal. The Rangers went on to defeat the Maroons in five games to win the Stanley Cup.

A New Era

The first all-NHL Stanley Cup was in 1927. It pitted the original Ottawa Senators against the Bruins. It was not the prettiest series in Stanley Cup history. Two of the games had to be suspended and declared as ties due to poor ice conditions. But the Senators won two games in the best-of-five series. That made them the first Stanley Cup champions in the modern NHL.

The first US champion in the new era was crowned in 1928. The Rangers defeated the Maroons in five games. Canadian center Frank Boucher

The Longest Game

The Detroit Red Wings won their first Stanley Cup in 1936. Getting to the finals was not easy. The Red Wings met the Montreal Maroons in a semifinal showdown. The game was tied at zero after regulation. The teams ended up playing six overtimes. Finally, after 116 minutes and 30 seconds, Moderre "Mud" Bruneteau scored the game-winner for Detroit. The Red Wings went on to sweep the series and move on to defeat the Toronto Maple Leafs for the Stanley Cup. But it was not before winning the longest game in Stanley Cup playoffs history through 2012.

led the Rangers with playoff highs of seven goals and three assists in nine games.

One year later, the Bruins and the Rangers met in the first Stanley Cup Finals without a Canadian team. Boston won its first title with a two-game sweep over the Rangers. The length of the series differed in the early years. The series was best-of-three in 1929 and 1930 before returning to best-of-five in 1931.

Even on the US teams, most of the players were Canadian. But the sport was rapidly growing in the United States. Six of the NHL's 10 teams were based in US cities. The league still had a strong presence in Canada,

The Toronto Maple Leafs, *in dark*, and the Boston Bruins battle each other for the Stanley Cup in 1939 in Toronto.

though. The Canadiens won the 1930 and 1931 Stanley Cups. Then it was Toronto's turn.

The Great Depression was causing tough financial times in the United States and Canada. Still, Smythe built a new arena for his team called Maple Leaf Gardens in 1931. It cost $1.5 million. That was an unthinkable price at the time. Just one year later, the Maple Leafs won their first Stanley Cup. They swept Smythe's former team, the Rangers, in three games. The Maple Leafs would soon become one of the most decorated teams in the NHL.

THE STANLEY CUP FINALS

"Mr. Zero"

The NHL grew after adding teams in larger US cities. Most of the early NHL players remained Canadian, though. Goaltender Frank Brimsek of Eveleth, Minnesota, became one of the first US-born stars in the game. As a rookie, he led the Boston Bruins to the 1939 Stanley Cup. He was also awarded the Vezina Trophy as the league's best goalie and the Calder Memorial Trophy as the league's best rookie that season. Brimsek also backstopped Boston to another Stanley Cup in 1941. He compiled 40 shutouts over his career, helping him earn the nickname "Mr. Zero."

The league continued to develop. Teams came and went. League formats were altered. And in 1938–39, the Stanley Cup Finals changed from a best-of-five to a best-of-seven series. That meant a team would need to win four games to claim the series. Every Stanley Cup Finals since has been a best-of-seven series.

The NHL was still a far cry from the league we know today. By the end of the 1930s, it had only seven teams. The Great Depression in the early-1930s made it hard for teams to make money. Then the United States entered World War II in 1941. By 1942, former NHL teams such as the Pittsburgh Pirates, the Montreal Maroons, and the New York Americans were gone. Only six teams remained.

Chapter 4

The Original Six Era

The Great Depression and World War II had taken their toll on the NHL in the early 1940s. Only the Boston Bruins, the Chicago Black Hawks, the Detroit Red Wings, the Montreal Canadiens, the New York Rangers, and the Toronto Maple Leafs made it through the tough financial times. They have become known as the "Original Six."

With only six teams, the top four in the standings qualified for the playoffs. The teams that came out on top in each series would then meet for the Stanley Cup.

Forward Syd Howe led the Detroit Red Wings to three Stanley Cup titles during his time there from 1935 and 1946.

The Greatest Dynasty

In 1960, the Montreal Canadiens swept the archrival Toronto Maple Leafs to win the Stanley Cup. It completed an amazing run in which Montreal won five consecutive Stanley Cup titles. The Habs, as they are sometimes known, played in every Stanley Cup Finals between 1951 and 1960. They won six Stanley Cups in that span, including the stretch of five straight. No team has ever repeated such a streak through 2012.

With so few teams, the Stanley Cup did not move around too much. Between 1943 and 1960, Detroit and Toronto each won five titles. Montreal was the most successful team in that era. It appeared in 13 of those 18 Stanley Cup Finals and won eight of them.

All Hail the Habs

The Canadiens of the 1940s and 1950s brought fame to the NHL with their superstar players and Stanley Cup dominance. At the heart of those Montreal teams was right wing Maurice "The Rocket" Richard. He joined the NHL in 1942–43, the first year of the Original Six era. Richard became the first player in NHL history to score 50 goals in one season in 1944–45. He was just 23 at the time. His blazing speed and dizzying skill made him an instant fan favorite.

THE STANLEY CUP FINALS

Right wing Maurice "The Rocket" Richard, *right,* led the Montreal Canadiens to eight Stanley Cup championships during his 18 seasons in the NHL.

Richard and his Canadiens appeared in every Stanley Cup Finals from 1951 to 1960. That turned many of Montreal's players into hockey celebrities. Richard retired in 1960 after winning his eighth Stanley Cup. He finished his career with 544 goals.

Then there was Bernie Geoffrion. The right wing earned the nickname "Boom Boom" for his powerful shot and physical play. Many credit him with inventing the slap shot. He did not miss a single Stanley Cup Finals game in his first eight seasons in the league with Montreal. Boom Boom was the second player to reach 50 goals in a season. He did so in 1961.

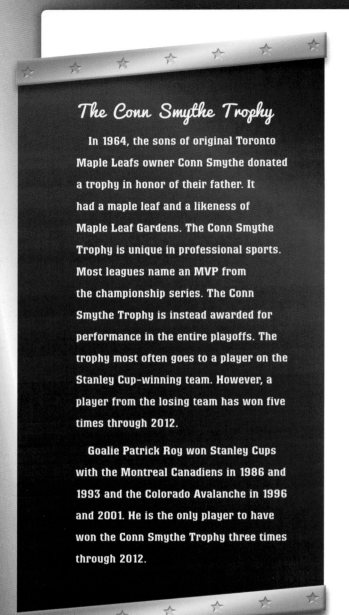

The Conn Smythe Trophy

In 1964, the sons of original Toronto Maple Leafs owner Conn Smythe donated a trophy in honor of their father. It had a maple leaf and a likeness of Maple Leaf Gardens. The Conn Smythe Trophy is unique in professional sports. Most leagues name an MVP from the championship series. The Conn Smythe Trophy is instead awarded for performance in the entire playoffs. The trophy most often goes to a player on the Stanley Cup-winning team. However, a player from the losing team has won five times through 2012.

Goalie Patrick Roy won Stanley Cups with the Montreal Canadiens in 1986 and 1993 and the Colorado Avalanche in 1996 and 2001. He is the only player to have won the Conn Smythe Trophy three times through 2012.

There was also the great center Jean Beliveau. He joined the Canadiens full-time in 1954. He led the team to the 1956 Stanley Cup, scoring 12 goals in the playoffs. Beliveau won 10 Stanley Cups and scored 507 goals over his 20-year career. All came with Montreal. He was also the first player to receive the Conn Smythe Trophy. It is given to the Stanley Cup playoffs Most Valuable Player (MVP) as voted by the media.

In 1955, Maurice Richard's younger brother Henri Richard joined the Habs. Henri Richard was just 19 years old. Each of his first five seasons ended with a Stanley Cup. Over his 20-year career, Henri Richard won 11 Stanley Cups with the Canadiens. That is the most of any player in the trophy's history through 2012.

THE STANLEY CUP FINALS

Mr. Hockey

The Canadiens had plenty of stars. They did not have the man who would become known to hockey fans across the world as "Mr. Hockey."

Gordie Howe entered the NHL as an 18-year-old in 1946. The young rising star had to watch his Red Wings win the 1950 Stanley Cup from a hospital bed. He had fractured his skull after a Maple Leafs player checked him into the boards in the semifinals.

Two years later, Howe was back in the Stanley Cup Finals. This time he led the Red Wings to the Cup with seven points in the postseason. That included a four-game sweep over Montreal in the Stanley Cup Finals. He also helped the Red Wings win two more Stanley Cups in 1954 and 1955.

Howe went on to play in 1,767 NHL games and scored 801 goals over his career. However, he never won another Stanley Cup after age 27. Howe never lost that competitive spirit, though. Mr. Hockey played professionally until he was 51 years old, retiring in 1980.

New Generations

Maurice Richard retired after the 1960 Stanley Cup. That opened the door for some new teams to hoist the famous trophy.

The 1961 Black Hawks featured two budding superstars in forwards Bobby Hull and Stan Mikita. They became the first team to knock

Stanley's Bowl Retired

The original Stanley Cup bowl was getting old and beat up by 1962. The Toronto Maple Leafs claimed the trophy that year. Afterward, the Hockey Hall of Fame retired the original bowl and collar. It was kept on display in the Hockey Hall of Fame until 1970, when it was stolen. It had been missing for seven years. Then an anonymous tipster notified police of where they could find it. The original bowl is back on display at the Hockey Hall of Fame in Toronto, resting in Lord Stanley's Vault.

Montreal out of the playoffs before the Stanley Cup Finals in more than a decade. And then the Black Hawks beat Detroit four games to two in the finals. For the first time in 20 years, the Stanley Cup ended up somewhere besides Toronto, Montreal, or Detroit.

Hull and Mikita each went on to Hall of Fame careers. But the 1961 Stanley Cup was their first and last. It was also the last Stanley Cup for Chicago until 2010. Meanwhile, the NHL's three traditional powers came right back to dominate. Toronto won the next three Stanley Cups. Then Montreal took two in a row before Toronto won again in 1967.

The 1967 season was significant for another reason. The NHL was hoping to acquire a more lucrative national television contract in the United States. So the league voted to add six new expansion teams in 1967–68.

The Original Six era had officially ended. The league was now twice as large. In addition, all of the new teams were placed in a separate division. Now four teams from each division would reach the playoffs. The playoffs also added a third round for the first time. Most significant, however, was the Stanley Cup. Now the champions from each division would meet in the Stanley Cup Finals. That meant there could no longer be a thrilling final series between two Original Six teams.

The Canadiens were quick to remind everyone who the top dog was. They won the first two Stanley Cups after expansion. Both times Montreal swept the St. Louis Blues in the finals. The Original Six would maintain a stranglehold on the Stanley Cup for a few more seasons. But times were changing in the NHL in a big way.

Chapter 5

The Expansion Era

Boston Bruins defenseman Bobby Orr was taking the league by storm in the late 1960s. He had a playing style unlike anyone had ever seen before. In 1969–70, Orr became the first defenseman to lead the NHL in scoring. He then led the Bruins to the Stanley Cup.

Orr had 20 points in 14 postseason games. Among those points was the overtime game-winning goal in Game 4 of the Stanley Cup Finals against the St. Louis Blues. Forty seconds into overtime, Orr skated with the puck across the Blues' crease and flicked the puck into the back

Boston Bruins defenseman Bobby Orr flies through the air after scoring the game-winning goal in overtime of Game 4 of the 1970 Stanley Cup Finals.

Broad Street Bullies

The Philadelphia Flyers became the first expansion team to win the Stanley Cup when they won in 1974 and 1975. Many around the league thought the Flyers played dirty to try to intimidate their opponents. A local newspaper called the Flyers "The Broad Street Bullies" in a 1973 headline. The name stuck. The biggest bully of them all may have been Dave "The Hammer" Schultz. He still held the record for most penalty minutes in a single season through 2012. He had 472 in 1974–75.

of the net. As Orr raised his hands to celebrate, he was tripped and went airborne. The scene was captured in one of sports' most famous photographs. The Bruins had won their first Stanley Cup since 1941.

New Teams, New Winners

The Bruins and the Canadiens traded spots as champion for the next three years. But a new professional league called the World Hockey Association (WHA) formed in 1972. Teams were sprouting up across the United States and Canada. Some big stars from the NHL were signing contracts with the new WHA. It appeared that the WHA might become a threat to the NHL. But ultimately the NHL always had one thing the WHA did not: the Stanley Cup.

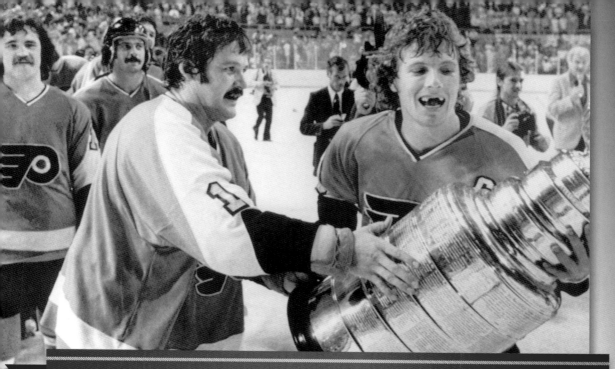

Bernie Parent, *left*, Bobby Clarke, *right*, and the "Broad Street Bullies" of the Philadelphia Flyers claimed their second straight Stanley Cup in 1975.

The NHL added six more teams between 1970 and 1974. That helped the league maintain superiority over the WHA. It also made winning a Stanley Cup even tougher.

Since the NHL expanded in 1967–68, Original Six teams had won every Stanley Cup through 1973. But the new teams were getting stronger. The Philadelphia Flyers were gaining notoriety around the league in the early 1970s. They were very physical—some say nasty—on the ice. That earned them the nickname "Broad Street Bullies." The name came from the road their arena was on.

Great Scotty

Scotty Bowman led the St. Louis Blues to the Stanley Cup Finals in each of his first three seasons as coach, from 1968 to 1970. But they lost all three times. In fact, St. Louis did not win a single game in any of those three series. That did not discourage Bowman, though. He made it back to the Stanley Cup Finals many times in his 30-year coaching career. In fact, Bowman led three different teams to the title. He won a record nine Stanley Cups as a head coach.

His greatest success was with the Montreal Canadiens. Bowman led them to the 1973 title before guiding them on a run of four straight between 1976 and 1979. In 1992, Bowman led the Pittsburgh Penguins to their second straight Stanley Cup. His final nine seasons were with the Detroit Red Wings. Bowman guided the team to Stanley Cup titles in 1997, 1998, and 2002.

By 1973–74, the Flyers were one of the NHL's best teams. The tougher road to the Stanley Cup barely slowed them down. Philadelphia swept the Atlanta Flames and then beat the New York Rangers in seven games. Then it pounded its way past Boston four games to two in the Stanley Cup Finals. That made the Flyers the first expansion team to win the Cup. Then they did it again the next year.

Center Bobby Clarke was Philadelphia's captain in those seasons. He provided a fitting image for the Broad Street Bullies with his grin that exposed his missing two front teeth.

The Flyers lost in the Stanley Cup Finals in 1976.

The Playoff Beard

Many players in the Stanley Cup playoffs choose not to shave. They often grow beards or goatees for good luck. It is believed that the tradition began in 1980 with the New York Islanders. The players do not shave their beards until they are knocked out of the playoffs or win the Stanley Cup.

That began a stretch in which the Canadiens once again dominated the NHL. They closed out the 1970s with four straight Stanley Cups. Dynamic goal-scoring right wing Guy Lafleur was the team's star. He led the playoffs in points in 1977, 1978, and 1979.

A New Dynasty

The WHA folded after that 1978–79 season. Four of those teams found a new home in the NHL. With 21 teams, the NHL changed its playoffs to include 16 teams. Once again the NHL had made it harder to win the Stanley Cup. But once again a dominant team emerged.

The New York Islanders entered the NHL in 1972. Al Arbour took over as coach in 1973. He began assembling what would soon be a powerhouse hockey team. The Islanders had many great teams during the 1970s. However, they always fell just short of the Stanley Cup Finals.

The team finally got its shot in 1980. Behind dynamic defenseman Denis Potvin and talented scorers Bryan Trottier and Mike Bossy, the Islanders reached the Stanley Cup Finals. With a four-games-to-two victory over Philadelphia, a new dynasty had begun. The Islanders won the next three Stanley Cups as well. They became the first expansion team dynasty in the NHL. And through 2012, no team had won four straight Stanley Cups since the Islanders.

The Great One

The Edmonton Oilers were one of the Islanders' Stanley Cup Finals victims. The Islanders swept the former WHA team in the 1983 Finals. But Edmonton was clearly up and coming. The Oilers were one of the most exciting teams in hockey. Plus, they featured a talented young forward from Brantford, Ontario, who wore No. 99 on his back.

That man was Wayne Gretzky. The man later known as "The Great One" led the Oilers back to the Stanley Cup Finals in 1984. This time they beat the Islanders four games to one. Gretzky posted seven points in the final series.

"Our dreams and thoughts were always to one day lift this trophy," Gretzky said. "When you do, it's a fact and no one can ever take that away from you."

The Edmonton Oilers' Wayne Gretzky skates against the New York Islanders during the 1984 Stanley Cup Finals.

The win also began a streak of success that nearly matched that of the Islanders. Gretzky was in the midst of an utterly dominant streak of his own. He led the NHL in assists every season from 1979–80 to 1991–92. He was the league's leading goal scorer every year but one from 1981–82 to 1986–87. He still held several scoring records in 2012. Yet Gretzky was not alone. The Oilers also featured dazzling Finnish forward Jari Kurri, slick-skating defenseman Paul Coffey, and athletic goalie Grant Fuhr.

In 1985, Gretzky set a playoffs record with 47 points in just 18 games. The Oilers beat the Flyers for another Cup. Montreal came back to win the 1986 Stanley Cup. Then Edmonton won two more in 1987 and 1988.

It was an unbelievable stretch. However, it ended with Gretzky being traded to the Los Angeles Kings.

Oilers fans were terribly upset. People across Canada felt betrayed by the move at first. However, Edmonton was not yet finished. Team captain Mark Messier led the Oilers to another Stanley Cup in 1990.

Super Mario

The Pittsburgh Penguins drafted a Canadian center named Mario Lemieux first in the 1984 NHL Draft. The Penguins had struggled to find success since joining the NHL in 1967. Many believed Lemieux would have the same effect on Pittsburgh that Gretzky had on Edmonton.

Lemieux was a star. His 199-point season in 1988–89 was considered one of the best ever. However, the Penguins made the playoffs just once in Lemieux's first six seasons. They made it for a second time in 1991. And that time they made it all the way to the Stanley Cup Finals.

A severe back injury forced Lemieux to sit out Game 3. When he returned the Penguins were down two games to one against the Minnesota North Stars. Then Lemieux put together a historic run. He led the Penguins to three straight wins and their first Stanley Cup. Lemieux scored five goals in his four Finals games en route to winning the Conn Smythe Trophy.

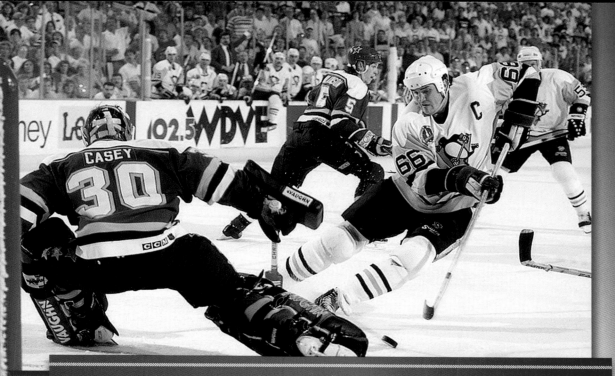

Mario Lemieux of the Pittsburgh Penguins tries to make a move against Minnesota North Stars goalie Jon Casey during the 1991 Stanley Cup Finals.

Lemieux led the Penguins to a second straight Stanley Cup in 1992. Pittsburgh swept the Chicago Blackhawks in four games. And Lemieux also won another Conn Smythe Trophy. Injuries and sickness occasionally slowed Lemieux throughout his career. But after those 1992 Finals, he had firmly established himself as one of the Stanley Cup's all-time greats.

Chapter 6

Still Making History

The 1990s were a time of change in the NHL. In 1993, the Montreal Canadiens won their twenty-fourth Stanley Cup. No other team had won more than 13. Then center Mark Messier and defenseman Brian Leetch led the New York Rangers to their tenth Stanley Cup in 1994. It was their first in 54 years. And with his playoff-leading 34 points, Leetch became the first US-born player to win the Conn Smythe Trophy.

Soon, however, new teams in new cities began making life harder for the Original Six powers. By 1996, the NHL had grown to 26 teams.

New York Rangers center Mark Messier celebrates after scoring against the Vancouver Canucks in Game 7 of the 1994 Stanley Cup Finals.

New teams began popping up in non-traditional hockey areas, such as Florida and Southern California. Other teams began moving to bigger US cities in an attempt to grow the league.

In 1995–96, the Quebec Nordiques moved to Denver and became the Colorado Avalanche. It turned out to be perfect timing. The team featured star centers Joe Sakic and Peter Forsberg and goalie Patrick Roy. They led the Avalanche to the Stanley Cup in their first season, beating the three-year-old Florida Panthers.

Detroit Dynasty

Another Original Six team ended a Stanley Cup drought the next year. It had been 42 years since the Detroit Red Wings had won a championship. Their last titles had come during the period in which the

Red Wings, Canadiens, and Toronto Maple Leafs won all but one Stanley Cup between 1942 and 1969.

Stanley Cup dynasties were all but extinct by 1997. After all, the league had grown to 26 teams. But the Red Wings became the closest thing to a dynasty since the 1980s Edmonton Oilers. Behind center Steve Yzerman, defenseman Nicklas Lidstrom, and others, Detroit swept the Philadelphia Flyers for the 1997 title. It was Detroit's first Stanley Cup since 1955. Then the Red Wings did it again, sweeping the Washington Capitals

Keepers of the Cup

Wherever the Stanley Cup goes, the Keepers go too. The Keepers are employees of the Hockey Hall of Fame in Toronto. It is their responsibility to accompany the Cup no matter where it goes. Every player on the winning team gets 24 hours with the Cup in the offseason. That makes for a very busy summer for hockey's ultimate prize and the people who keep it safe. With more than 300 public engagements a year, the Stanley Cup and its Keepers log a lot of frequent flyer miles.

for the 1998 Stanley Cup. Yzerman led all players with 24 playoff points en route to winning the Conn Smythe Trophy.

Detroit fell short in the playoffs over the next three seasons. The 2001–02 Red Wings were back, though. The team still featured core players such as Yzerman and Lidstrom. Meanwhile, it had added other superstars including right wing Brett Hull, left wing Luc Robitaille, defenseman Chris Chelios, and center Pavel Datsyuk. The powerful Red Wings simply outmatched the upstart Carolina Hurricanes. Detroit won its tenth Stanley Cup in just five games.

The Red Wings were not quite as dominant as the Islanders and the Oilers had been in the 1980s. But from 1993 to 2012, only the New Jersey Devils and the Avalanche also won two Stanley Cups in a six-year span.

"The sheer joy of winning, raising the Cup, that's the only reason you play," said Yzerman in 1997. "I did it for the nine-year-old kid in me and the kid in all of these wonderful Detroit fans who have waited so long for this day."

Rocky Mountain Good Times

Defenseman Ray Bourque had become one of the NHL's best during his long career with the Boston Bruins. He had accomplished almost everything one can in the league. The only thing that was missing was a Stanley Cup.

In 2000, he requested and received a trade to the Avalanche. He joined with Forsberg, Sakic, and Roy to make a top team. But they fell just short in the playoffs that year. Still, Bourque decided to give it one more try. He returned to the Avalanche for the 2000–01 season at age 40.

This time the Avalanche reached the Stanley Cup Finals. But Bourque and the Avs soon found themselves down three games to two against the Devils. It looked as though Bourque would fall short of his goal. That was until the Avs won the next two games to win the Cup.

It is custom that the winning team's captain lifts the Stanley Cup above his head first. But Avalanche captain Sakic did not. Instead he passed it to Bourque, allowing the old veteran the chance to live out his boyhood dream. Bourque retired after that season.

It was a tough loss for the Devils. However, they too were one of the NHL's best teams of that era. Behind goalie Martin Brodeur, they won the Stanley Cup in 1995, 2000, and again in 2003.

New Teams, Old Teams

The NHL took a risk when it put teams in cities with warmer climates during the 1990s. Indeed, some of those teams struggled to find fan bases. Others had more success.

In 1999, the Dallas Stars became the southernmost Stanley Cup champion in NHL history. By 2000, there were 30 teams in the NHL from coast to coast. In 2004, the Tampa Bay Lightning lifted the Stanley Cup in Florida. Then it was the Carolina Hurricanes—based in Raleigh, North Carolina—in 2006. For the first time in 90 years, the Stanley Cup returned to the West Coast in 2007. That year the Anaheim Ducks beat the Ottawa Senators for California's first Stanley Cup.

Veteran Colorado Avalanche defenseman Ray Bourque raises the Stanley Cup over his head for the first and only time in his 22-year career in 2001.

Just as new markets were starting to win Stanley Cups, the Red Wings, Chicago Blackhawks, and Boston Bruins won three of the four Stanley Cups from 2008 to 2011. In 2008, Lidstrom became the first European-born and trained player to captain a team to the Stanley Cup. Six years earlier, he was the first European to win the Conn Smythe Trophy.

Stanley Cup Mystery

Chicago Blackhawks right wing Patrick Kane scored the Stanley Cup–clinching goal in Game 6 in 2010. But it happened so fast even the television announcers were not sure if it was a goal. Kane's low shot went through Philadelphia Flyers goalie Michael Leighton. It got lodged under the white padding at the bottom of the net. Kane knew it was in, but almost nobody else did.

After video review, it was confirmed a goal. The game was over and the Blackhawks had won the Stanley Cup. However, when the Hockey Hall of Fame went to retrieve the puck, it was nowhere to be found. There are many theories about where it went and who has it. But no one has come forward. Even the FBI got in on the investigation, with no success. Perhaps this will remain a Stanley Cup mystery for the ages.

Detroit's 2008 win helped cement that team as one of the best of its generation. The Chicago and Boston wins, meanwhile, ended long droughts. The Blackhawks ended a 49-year Stanley Cup drought in 2010. The Bruins won their first Cup in 39 years in 2011.

The Kings made a miraculous playoff run for another California Stanley Cup in 2012. They entered the playoffs seeded eighth in their conference. But seemingly nobody could get the puck past Kings goalie Jonathan Quick. The Kings rolled through the playoffs and Stanley Cup Finals

with only four losses. No eighth-seeded team had ever won the Stanley Cup until then.

The Stanley Cup has always been a coveted trophy that is hard to win. It has only gotten harder in recent years. Now the postseason lasts close to eight weeks after a grueling 82-game regular season. But for the champions and their fans, the journey is always worth it if it ends with Lord Stanley's Cup above the captain's head.

TIMELINE

Lord Stanley purchases a silver bowl from a silversmith in London and calls it the Dominion Challenge Trophy.
1892

Montreal AAA compiles a 7–1–0 record to finish as champion of the AHAC, making it the first team to win the Dominion Challenge Trophy.
1893

The first all-professional Stanley Cup final series is held. The Toronto Blueshirts of the NHA win.
1914

The Montreal Canadiens win their first Stanley Cup. Over the next 90 years, the Canadiens would win 23 more Stanley Cups.
1916

The Seattle Metropolitans defeat the Montreal Canadiens to become the first American-based team to win the Stanley Cup.
1917

The NHL adds six teams, which form the West Division. The 1968 Stanley Cup Finals pit winners of the West Division against the winners of the East Division.
1967

The Philadelphia Flyers become the first expansion team to capture the Stanley Cup. They win again in 1975.
1974

The WHA, a professional league competing with the NHL, ceases operations. The NHL absorbs four WHA teams.
1979

With its fourth consecutive Stanley Cup, the New York Islanders become just the third team in NHL history to win more than three in a row.
1983

The Edmonton Oilers win their second straight Stanley Cup as Wayne Gretzky sets the record for most points in a single Stanley Cup playoffs with 47.
1985

The NHA ceases operations and the NHL is formed. The Toronto Arenas defeat the Vancouver Millionaires to win the Stanley Cup.

1918

The Western Hockey League, formerly the WCHL, ceases operations, making the NHL the only professional league remaining.

1926

The NHL introduces the best-of-seven playoff format. The Boston Bruins defeat the Toronto Maple Leafs four games to one for the Stanley Cup.

1939

After financial troubles caused the other teams to fold, six teams remain. They later become known as "The Original Six."

1942

The Conn Smythe Trophy is awarded for the first time. Jean Beliveau of the Montreal Canadiens is the first recipient.

1965

Mark Messier and Brian Leetch lead the New York Rangers to their first Stanley Cup in 54 years. Leetch becomes the first US Conn Smythe Award winner.

1994

The Dallas Stars become the southernmost team to win the Stanley Cup.

1999

Legendary coach Scotty Bowman retires after guiding the Detroit Red Wings to the Stanley Cup. It is his ninth as a head coach, a Stanley Cup record.

2002

The Anaheim Ducks become the western-most team to win the Stanley Cup since the Seattle Metropolitans 90 years earlier.

2007

Sidney Crosby leads the Pittsburgh Penguins to the Stanley Cup title over the Detroit Red Wings.

2009

CHAMPIONSHIP OVERVIEW

The Trophy

Donated by Frederick Arthur Stanley, Lord of Preston, in 1892, the Stanley Cup is now awarded to the NHL's playoff champion. The championship team's roster is inscribed on the body of the Stanley Cup, which stands 35.25 inches (89.54 cm) and weighs 34.5 pounds (15.65 kg).

The Legends

Jean Beliveau (Montreal Canadiens): 10 Stanley Cups, one MVP

Wayne Gretzky (Edmonton Oilers): Four Stanley Cups, two MVPs

Bobby Orr (Boston Bruins): Two Stanley Cups, two MVPs

Maurice Richard (Montreal Canadiens): Eight Stanley Cups

Patrick Roy (Montreal Canadiens and Colorado Avalanche): Four Stanley Cups, three MVPs

The Victors

Montreal Canadiens: 24 since 1916

Toronto Maple Leafs: 13 since 1918

Detroit Red Wings: 11 since 1936

Ottawa Senators (original): 11 from 1903 to 1927

Boston Bruins: 6 since 1929

GLOSSARY

amateur
An athlete who can not earn money for playing a sport.

archrival
The opposing team that brings out the greatest emotion from fans and players.

challenge cup
A trophy for which teams can challenge the defending champion.

commissioner
The lead administrator, or person in charge of a league.

dominion
A self-governing nation that is part of the United Kingdom. Canada was a dominion until the twentieth century.

draft
A system used by professional sports leagues to select new players in order to spread incoming talent among all teams. The NHL Draft is usually held in June.

dynasty
A team that wins many championships during a short period of time.

expansion
Adding a new team or teams to a league.

overtime
The time added to the end of a game if no winner is decided during regulation time.

FOR MORE INFORMATION

Selected Bibliography

Falla, Jack. *Quest for the Cup: A History of the Stanley Cup Finals 1893-2001*. San Diego, CA: Thunder Bay Press, 2001.

Gruneau, Richard, and David Whitson. *Hockey Night in Canada*. Toronto: Garamond Press, 1993.

McKinley, Michael. *Putting A Roof on Winter*. Vancouver, BC: Greystone, 2000.

NHL Public Relations Department. *National Hockey League Official Guide & Record Book 2011-12*. Chicago, IL: Triumph Books, 2011.

Zweig, Eric, James Duplacey, and Dan Diamond. *The Ultimate Prize: The Stanley Cup*. Kansas City, MO: Andrews McMeel, 2003.

Further Readings

Bernstein, Ross. *Raising Stanley: What it Takes to Claim Hockey's Ultimate Prize*. Chicago, IL: Triumph, 2010.

Keepers of the Cup. *Travels With Stanley*. Chicago, IL: Triumph, 2007.

McKinley, Michael. *Ice Time: The Story of Hockey*. Toronto: Tundra Books, 2006.

Sports Illustrated: The Hockey Book. New York: Sports Illustrated Books, 2010.

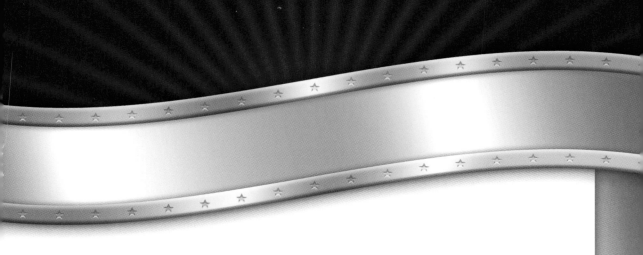

Web Links

To learn more about the Stanley Cup, visit ABDO Publishing Company online at **www.abdopublishing.com**. Web sites about the Stanley Cup are featured on our Book Links page. These links are routinely monitored and updated to provide the most current information available.

Places to Visit

Hockey Hall of Fame
30 Yonge Street, Toronto, ON M5E 1X8, Canada
(416) 360-7735
www.hhof.com
This hall of fame celebrates the history of hockey and its greatest players and contributors through memorabilia and other interactive exhibits. Among the highlights of the museum is the opportunity to view the original Stanley Cup trophy.

US Hockey Hall of Fame and Museum
801 Hat Trick Avenue, P.O. Box 679, Eveleth, MN 55734
(800) 443-7825
www.ushockeyhall.com
Located in northern Minnesota, this hall of fame and museum celebrates the history of US hockey through various exhibits. It also contains an ice rink.

INDEX

About the Author

Chris Peters is a freelance writer from Chicago. He has written feature stories for *USA Hockey Magazine*, USAHockey.com, and is editor of the hockey blog UnitedStatesofHockey.com. Prior to becoming a full-time writer, Peters worked in the communications department for USA Hockey. He currently resides with his wife in North Liberty, Iowa.